Community Heroes and Curious Explorers:
Investing with Time, Education, and the Power of Positive Impact!

Book 4 of the My First Finance Coloring Book Series

Written by: Ben Hofstetter and Nick Zehrung

TABLE OF CONTENTS

Part 1:

Community Heroes: Investing Time and Money for a Better Future

For Parents

Key Themes Explored in this chapter:

- In this chapter, we explore the significance of contributing to our community. We use the phrase "create a positive impact" to emphasize the reasons behind giving back and to distinguish it from the ways we generate income, such as "bringing value." By understanding the importance of making a positive difference, we can better appreciate the value of supporting and uplifting those around us.

- Different forms of giving back to the community are discussed, to include donating money, volunteering time, and the basic principles of a non-profit.

- Activity to try at home!: Organize a family donation drive where everyone contributes toys, clothes, or other items to donate to a local charity.

So far, we've learned about three ways to use our money: spending it on things we need or want, saving it for later, and investing it! Now, we're going to learn about another way to invest our money and our time - giving it back to our community!

Giving back means using our resources to help others and make a positive impact on our community. It can be as simple as donating toys, clothes, or money to those in need.

We can also volunteer our time to support local groups or participate in community projects.

In previous books we learned that by doing things that provide value to our community, we can earn money and make it a better place. But it's also important to know that we can make a positive impact on our community by helping others without expecting anything in return.

For example, you could help teach a classmate on a subject you are an expert in!

Remember when we had our lemonade stand? Our customers were thirsty people who wanted a refreshing drink. We provided value to them by getting all the supplies, making the drinks, and being available for them to buy from us.

They could have made their own lemonade, but we saved them time and effort, and that's why they were happy to pay us!

When we do something to help others who can't get what we're offering in any other way, it's called making a positive impact!

For example, someone might not have the money to pay for our lemonade. But if you give them a glass to cool off on a hot day, even though they can't pay you, you're making a positive impact on your community and that person's life!

When you give some of your money to local charities, you can make a difference for causes you care about, even if you can't directly help them yourself.

For example, you can donate $5 to a local pet shelter that will use it to provide food for a lonely puppy. By giving money to another organization, you're helping the puppy, showing your care, and making a positive impact in your community.

Did you know you can start a special kind of business that makes money to support the community? It's called a non-profit! Instead of keeping the money for themselves, non-profits give it all back to help others.

Imagine creating t-shirts with fun designs and selling them to raise money for something important to you. With this business, every dollar you earn will go towards making a positive impact in your community.

Volunteering is a fantastic way to make a difference in your community! You don't need to give money. Instead, you offer your time and help in amazing ways!

For instance, you could head to the local park and lend a hand by picking up trash. By doing this, you're showing how much you care about keeping your community clean and beautiful!

Now that we know how to make a difference in our community, let's discover why it's important to do so! One of the best reasons is the happiness and pride we feel when we make our community a better place.

When we help others, animals, or clean up the land, we can see the immediate impact we have on our community. It's an amazing feeling to see how beautiful a local forest becomes after we pick up the trash.

Another amazing benefit of providing a positive impact on your community is practicing the skills you'll need to be successful in your own businesses!

For instance, you could practice your sales skills in the t-shirt business, or practice your leadership skills while getting your friends together to clean the park!

Once you discover how amazing it feels to make a positive difference in your community, you won't want to stop! Your hard work and effort can make your neighborhood a better place to live. Keep going, and one day you'll see your area become even more wonderful!

Part 2:

Exploring New Horizons: Investing in Education and Learning

For Parents

Key Themes Explored in this chapter:

- In this chapter we explore the importance of education and continued learning. We discuss the rationale behind paying for a learning course and how that money is spent as an investment in your child's future. We also discuss how there are many free resources to explore, to include books and libraries as well as digital resources.

- The themes of "staying curious" and "constant learning" are used to show that gaining more knowledge will lead to finding new ways to bring value and provide a positive impact to your community.

- Activity to try at home!: Take a trip to a local library and encourage your child to borrow books that align with their interests. Discuss the value of reading and the knowledge they can gain from books.

Now that we've learned about four ways to use our money - spending, saving, investing in business, and donating - let's explore a fifth way: investing in our education and future!

Investing in education is all about using our resources to learn and grow. Just like we invest money to buy things, we can also invest in gaining knowledge and skills. It's like discovering a magical door that opens up a world of possibilities!

For instance, investing in this book and learning from it can help us unlock new knowledge and expand our horizons!

One way to invest in education is by taking special classes. Just like buying a toy, we can use some of our money to sign-up for exciting courses that teach us new things. It's like having a treasure chest full of knowledge!

On the next page we'll see an example!

Remember your friend who started a lawn mowing business? What if they offered a special class on how to become a lawn mowing expert like them? By taking their course, you can learn how to mow the best lawns in town and start your very own business!

If you're interested in learning about specific new skills, investing in a course about those skills is a great option!

Investing in education doesn't always mean spending money. We can also invest our time in free learning opportunities!

Exploring libraries, reading books, and discovering information online are like planting seeds of knowledge that grow and blossom over time!

In today's age, investing in digital skills is crucial. Learning how to navigate the internet safely, coding basics, and using technology responsibly can open doors to exciting opportunities and future careers.

And the best part is, you can learn these skills for free and then use them to make money!!

When we invest in education, we become curious explorers and lifelong learners. We gain new skills, discover our passions, and become more confident in ourselves. Education is like a magical power that helps us unlock doors to a bright future!

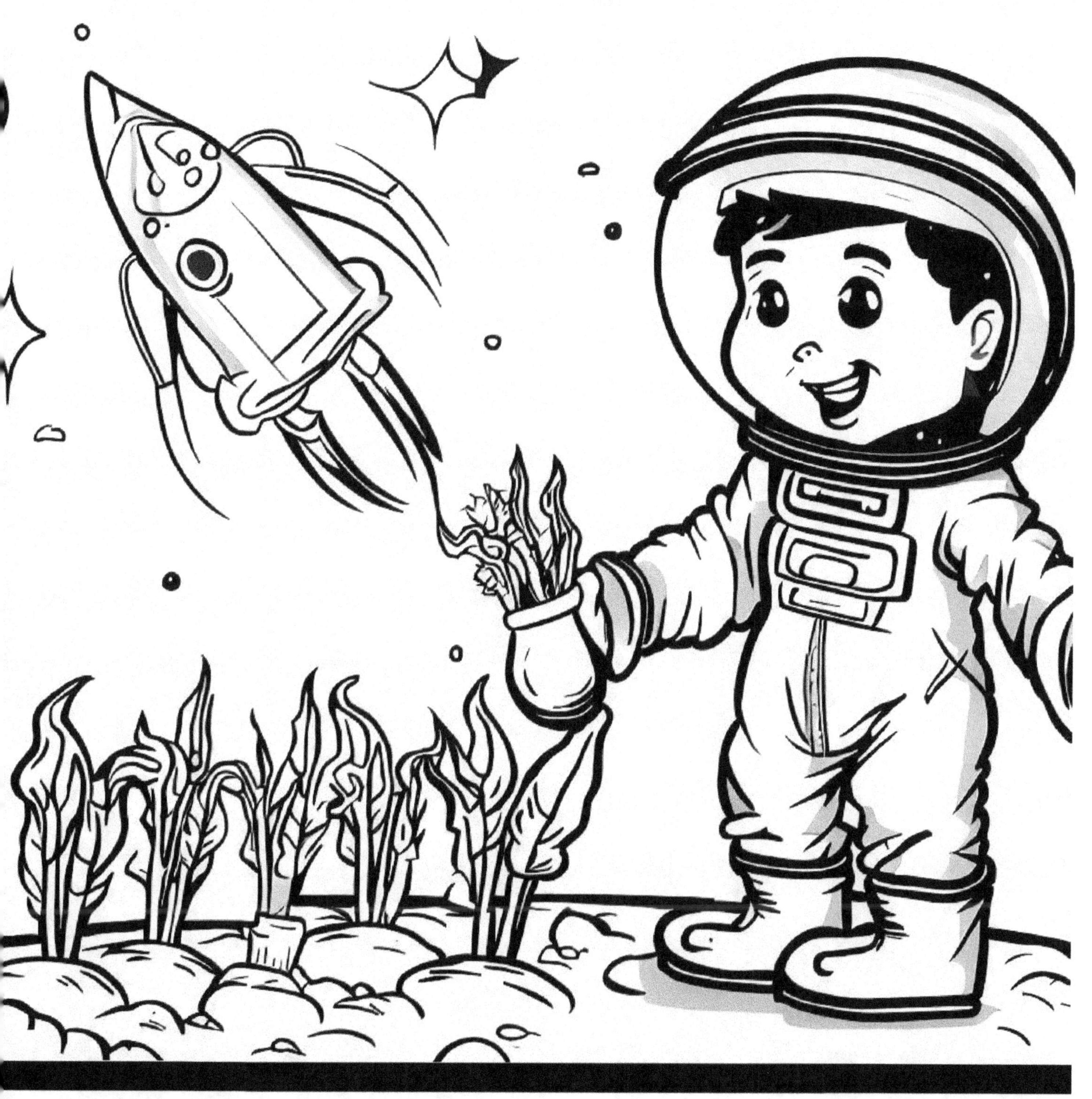

Remember, as long as you're continuing to learn, there isn't a door that will be closed to you! You'll always be able to find a way to bring value to the community you are a part of and find a home, maybe even out among the stars!

Thank you for joining us on this adventure in Book 1 of the "My First Finance Coloring Book" series!

We hope you loved learning about personal finance and wish to continue on the journey towards financial literacy with us.

The next step is Book 5: "From Little Seeds to Great Fortunes: The Magic of Long Term Investing!" which is now available on Amazon along with the rest of the coloring book series!

We also have a 3 book illustrated series available on Amazon for more advanced learners. It covers many of the same topics that are covered throughout the coloring book series, but at a more detailed level! The first book is titled "Money Magic: A Kid's Book Exploring Earning, Saving, and Budgeting While Having Fun!"

If you wish to support us and our goal to bring financial literacy to the next generation, there's two easy steps.

1) Follow us on Instagram @myfirstfinancebook
2) Leave a review on Amazon so others can find us too!
3) Reach out with questions at
 https://www.myfirstfinancebook.com

Thank you again for coloring your way through this book and we hope to see you soon! - The Authors